THINK.
GROW.
LIVE.

To Mairead.

Thank you for showing
an interest.

Thank you.

Davil Bren

THINK.
GROW.
LIVE.

DANIEL BRENNAN

ISBN-13: 978-0 9931143-6-6

ISBN-10: 0993114369

To find out more about Daniel Brennan and his approach to living, visit *www.danielbrennan.eu* or *www.uyplifestyle.com*.

DROMBEG BOOKS, IRELAND

CONTENTS

INTRODUCTION

Think. Grow. Live

I guess I'm a little different from a lot of twenty-year-olds, but I have come to realize that different is good, within reason.

Growing up in a town in the south-west of Ireland, I have had an incredible upbringing. I come from a great home where my parents have provided everything I have ever needed and more, a lot more. They have supported me in ways you can't imagine, and I am extremely grateful for that. I have gone through periods when I haven't been so grateful but I believe that that's all part of growing up and learning.

I have spent most of the past six years working on my golf game and trying to figure things out. My main question was, how could I become a better golfer? Golf is my passion and it always will be. My venture into self-development and trying to better myself as a person was initially, I must admit, an attempt to better my golf, but it has gone far beyond that now and it feeds into all areas of my life. I spent a year in the United States on a golf scholarship, and that was a huge learning curve for me. It didn't go as planned, but that's okay, and I am now realizing the benefits of the experience. Some people may say I have failed by not doing my four years, but I firmly believe that what is meant for you won't pass you by. I got a bit lost in the States and the life was a little too enjoyable for me. I made some bad decisions in college but I'm okay with that because it has all helped me get to where I am right now, and I wouldn't want to be anywhere else.

Sometimes my family may think I'm a bit over the top and extreme, but that's good in my opinion. I spend hours and hours a day alone, practicing and working on my golf game, and this gives me a lot of time to think. Thinking is something we do, all day every day. Even when we are not consciously thinking, we are still thinking, still having subconscious conversations with ourselves, talking in our own heads. That's the basis for this book: to help you become more aware of the conversations in your head and also to help you make decisions that will help you achieve your goals.

I have not written this book with millions of dollars in my bank account or with a garage filled with super cars, but I have written it with the understanding of what it takes for me to be happy. I have goals and aspirations, and it's what I do on a day-to-day basis that helps me achieve them. I'm on a journey, life's journey, and that's exciting to me. It's exciting because

I don't know what comes next. The fun part about working towards a goal is the journey, and that's what I embrace and enjoy.

I got the idea of writing a book when I was sitting in the garden of a villa in Portugal reading Jack Canfield's book *The Success Principles*, in which he mentioned a college student who wrote a book at eighteen. Jack Canfield's books are incredible and have been a great source of encouragement and inspiration for me, as has been Daniel Doyle's *The Talent Code*, which I read when I was sixteen.

I have written this book with the intention of helping myself, but I feel also that I have some valuable information to share. The aim is to help anyone who wants to improve their lives. I didn't want this book to drag out, but to be short and to the point. The book has a small bit to do with sport, but it is generally directed at anybody who is seriously looking to improve themselves. Also, the book is like a breakfast buffet: you can take what you want from it and leave the bits that you don't think are important. I don't believe that everyone will agree one hundred per cent with everything I say, but if you take one per cent from the book, that's one per cent you never had before.

The message here is simple: *You can change*. I want to make people think — think about the world and think about the millions of incredible things they can do. Don't be afraid of what other people think. I used to be very afraid of what people thought of me, but your reputation is only a perception, your character is who you are.

"Be more concerned with your character than your reputation, because your character is what you really are, while your reputation is merely what others think you are." — *John Wooden, UCLA basketball coach 1948-1975.*

Although this book is aimed at any person who wants to make a change to their lives, I am trying to reach out in particular to those of my own age (we are all great people). We are the future and we can determine what happens with it. It's sad to admit, but already I have seen some friends with great potential waste their talent. But it's never too late to change, no matter what age you are. *And now is the time to do it.*

Work hard, live in the present and enjoy the journey. Stay hungry, stay humble!

MASTER YOUR THOUGHTS

▶ Your mind is your most precious resource, look after it.

▶ Take note of your thoughts. Awareness is the first step in change.

▶ Repetition is the key.

▶ Practice makes permanent, so practice the right thoughts.

▶ Your reality is only a perception of any given situation. It may or may not be true.

▶ Your mind is a flashlight; where you focus your thoughts, your mind will follow.

▶ By building a strong self-image, you are building a strong foundation.

▶ A strong self-image can go a long way to helping you become the person you want to be.

▶ Your thoughts can be your best friend or your worst enemy; its up to you to chose which you'd prefer.

"Your subconscious mind does not argue with you. It accepts what your conscious mind decrees. If you say, ' 'I can't afford it,' your subconscious mind works to make it true. Select a better thought. Decree, 'I'll buy it. I accept it in my mind.' — **Dr Joseph Murphy**, *The Power of Your Subconscious Mind.*

Overcoming negativity

The main problem with our thought processes, as Joseph Murphy points out, is that over the years we have become conditioned to thinking negatively. Thoughts like, " I can't do that"or "I'm not good enough", when repeated enough, take root in our subconscious as part of our belief system about ourselves and thus become self-fulfilling. On the other hand, the ability to talk to yourself in a positive, affirmative voice will help your confidence tremendously and put you on the path towards achieving your dreams.

I believe that self-talk and affirmations play a huge part in positive thinking and mastering your own thoughts and ultimately your own destiny. From my own experience, self-talk and being aware of your thoughts is the key to happiness. Your thoughts determine how you experience every single thing in the world, so why not have total control over them?

Self-talk is powerful. It helps you believe that you are or will be the person you want to become. It will also teach you to perceive situations in a more positive manner, provided you give your mind the positivity it deserves. Mindfulness is the key, and being mindful of your thoughts gives you the ability to correct your thinking.

> Mindfulness is the key and being mindful of your thoughts gives you the ability to correct your thinking.

I believe that your thoughts control everything that you do in your life. They do *not* control everything that happens to you, but they *do* control everything you do. Knowing the difference between the two gives you great control over your thinking and how you react to circumstances.

Let's get started.

More people work hard on improving their bodies and their image rather than on their thoughts. This baffles me because it is our thoughts that determine how we experience life, and the simple fact is that if we don't manage them, they will manage us. Think of your

9

thoughts as your body. If you neglect your body for a year and don't exercise or eat healthily, how will you look and feel? Overweight, out of shape? Physically you'll feel awful. Your thoughts are no different. If you neglect them and don't look after them, they too will get out of shape and make you feel awful.

Think of how carefully athletes look after their bodies; we should do exactly the same with our minds. But how exactly?

Easy...work at it. Belief and a consistent work ethic are the way to achieve most goals you set yourself, whether physical or mental. The first objective is to become more alert and be able to monitor your thoughts; once you can do that, you can then master them. Mastering your thoughts doesn't mean you don't have negative thoughts, it just means that when you start to think negatively, you see the thought for what it is, discard it and then replace it with the opposite.

Mastering your thoughts sounds daunting, but it isn't. It's just choosing what is right for you, your goals and your mind. It's like going shopping and instead of buying chocolate and soft drinks you buy vegetables and nutrient-rich foods. It means choosing what you know is best for you, not what's easiest. Once you have gone to the store to pick up the foods that are good for you, the next time you go back it will be that little bit easier to choose the good foods again. The same goes for your thoughts. Repetition helps to make a habit permanent, good or bad.

Take note

You can't fix something if you don't know it is broken, so in the effort to master your thoughts, you must first become aware of them. Take a note of your thoughts throughout the day. Do this for a week; anytime you think something and realize "I am aware that I thought this", write it down. This simple step is the first step towards realizing how you think. This is just to build awareness and to discover the level of change needed. Don't fool yourself by writing down only positive thoughts; also write down all the negative thoughts you become aware of during the day. Don't think that writing down all those negative thoughts is a bad thing; it's just the start of the process of changing your diet for your mind. Writing down any positive thoughts you have will only reinforce your good beliefs about yourself.

Don't think at all that it's strange that you're doing

this exercise. Yes, it's different, but in order to be un-like everybody else, you must think unlike everybody else. If you want to be great, you must think great. If you want to be a billionaire, you must think like a billionaire. Your mind will allow you to do, or not do, anything you tell it.

The next step

The next step is to change the negative thoughts with their opposites. We can't go back in time, but when a particular negative thought pops up again you will now be more aware, and all you have to do is think, "I can choose to feed this thought or I can discard it and swap it for a new, positive thought." Discarding and swapping the thought is naturally always the best option. You may not get all of this right at the beginning, of course, but if you work consistently at it you will soon have mastery over every thought or visualization that comes into your mind.

One way to help you reach your goal of full control over your thoughts is through the use of affirmations,

One way to help you reach your goal of full control over your thoughts is through the use of affirmations.

which are simply positive sayings, phrases or sentences that you say to yourself (as many times as you like) throughout the day. Affirmations are a great way to stay positive and to get your day off to a great start. They can also help you believe in yourself and in your abilities. Many top athletes and entrepreneurs say they have used affirmations to change and better their lives. How? Affirmations change your subconscious way of thinking. What you believe about yourself and the world around you hasn't happened overnight. It may have taken a week, a year or ten years, but what you believe about yourself is merely an opinion that you have created.

Affirmations can positively change that opinion from "I can't do that" to "of course, I can do that". Or "I'm not talented enough" to "I am talented enough and talent is overrated, hard work is the key". Affirmations can trick your brain into believing you are something that you're not, and this is vital to becoming a successful person in whatever you want to achieve. Affirmations affect that little chatterbox in your head, but in a positive way.

If you read your own affirmations several times a day, you will see a huge improvement in how things hap-

13

pen to you. Not because the situations have changed but because your perception of any given situation will change. It is also important to remember that even if you don't believe at first what your affirmations say about you, keep at it. You will soon believe it entirely.

How do you write your own affirmations? The best way I can answer that is to share with you one of my affirmations that I read every morning. I know that I am publicly showing people what I say to myself, but that's okay. What is also okay is keeping your affirmations completely private. I know and I have experienced the sense of embarrassment when someone reads my affirmations without me wanting them to. It isn't nice, so keep them discreet if you must.

"I am grateful for waking up this morning. I am blessed to have another day to conquer. Today I will trust myself in my process of improvement. I am improving every single day, in life and in golf. GOOD MORNING WORLD. Yes, it will be a great morning and a great day. I enter today with an attitude of appreciation for everything I have in my life and everything that is yet to come. I am changing every second, for the better. I am at peace within my mind and I am so lucky to have another day to pursue my dream. I am going out today to be grateful, work hard and rule

my thoughts. I will IMPROVE. I am already the greatest. Thank you."

This is my morning affirmation and I read it as early as I can every day. I have other affirmations that I read to reinforce great thoughts even more, which I will share in later chapters.

You can't build a house without a foundation, so don't try and build a belief without a foundation either. Affirmations are part of your foundation, so make them a part of your life.

Self-image

Your self-image is the mental image you have made up of yourself. It can be influenced and even changed by your opinion of yourself and other people's opinions of you, or how you think other people perceive you. Although it might be true, your self-image is completely made up.

Depending on how you see yourself can influence how you see the world around you also. Affirmations and self-talk can influence your self-image in a very positive way. Although some people may think you're delusional if you read affirmations or think in a posi-

15

tive manner, you are only doing what is good for you and your goals. You can work on and improve your image of yourself by doing the correct things.

Your mind is a flashlight

Imagine yourself in a dark room. The only thing you have is a flashlight. When you turn on the flashlight, it gives you a beam of light in whatever direction you point it.

Your mind is no different. You can use it to search for something positive or something negative. Direct it towards the negative and you'll get negative results, towards the positive and you'll get positive results. Think of your mind as a flashlight that you can control and point always in the right direction.

Reality or not?

What is reality? It varies from person to person. But isn't reality, REAL? Not entirely. Some things are certainly real, like gravity, which doesn't change from person to person, but in other areas of life thoughts of reality change between each individual. I might perceive something completely differently to how you perceive it. Many of my family and friends think that my dropping out of college is a bad choice, because their reality is, "You must go to school to get a good job." Simply, their reality of this situation is different to mine.

You build your own reality through how you think, and that is why I'm putting such an emphasis on mastering your thoughts and being aware. You will simply create a better and more enjoyable reality for yourself. You'll also begin to realize how many people's realities are bad because their thoughts reflect them. Change your reality to the reality that you want to have, not the reality your parents, friends or family have for you. It's YOUR reality for a reason.

Think great to be great

Thinking great thoughts is an incredible feeling. With the ability to think great, you can be great. You can become who or what you want to become. Mastering your thoughts makes the difference between working hard and slacking off, eating healthily or eating badly, being happy or being unhappy, and even being rich or being poor.

Build your thoughts so that you can benefit any areas of your life that you want to improve. If you want to

17

be great at sport, tell yourself you are great at sport. If you want to work harder, tell yourself to work harder. Hard-wire whatever great beliefs that you think you need. Identifying these can be difficult, but if you can be brutally honest, it can be easy. Focus your thoughts in a way that won't allow negative thoughts to become a part of your being. Allow yourself to be free. Structure your life around positivity, productivity and character. Combine these three, and you have no option but to succeed.

THE ONLY MOMENT IS NOW

▶ The only moment really is now.

▶ Physically, the only place you can be is where you are right now.

▶ Cycles happen every moment of our lives; it's what you choose to do in each cycle that determines what person you will be in the next cycle.

▶ Your thoughts may be crazy, but they will settle.

▶ Take ten minutes a day to look after your mind.

▶ Your mind determines how you perceive everything; looking after it may change your entire life.

▶ The ability to achieve anything begins with one simple thought.

"That day, I suddenly realized that I was no longer driving consciously, and I was in a different dimension. The circuit for me was a tunnel and I realized that I was well beyond my conscious understanding." — **Ayrton Senna**, Formula One driver

What is this moment?

What are you doing this very moment? Right now, I'm typing this book. I can hear people talking around me. I can feel the chair that I'm sitting on and the music in the background. I am aware, and this is the *moment*. The moment is the most underrated but special place that we can be. Right now it is the only place that you can physically be, so why choose to be somewhere else mentally?

Two ways to get into the moment are through meditation and becoming more aware of your thoughts. There is a great TED Talk by Andy Puddicomb that explains being present extremely well.

The pace of our lives is so quick and fast, when do we ever take time for ourselves? Being in this moment is being blank. And being blank means fully blank. Blank doesn't mean having just one or two thoughts.

Blank means no thoughts. Blank means not reminiscing about the past or thinking about the future. When you can start to be blank, you will start to realize patterns in your thinking. You will realize that maybe you are too laid back, or too intense. If there is something small bugging you, you can fix it. But first, you have to be aware of it. Being mindful will help you realize that "every time I try to be blank, this one thing keeps coming up more and more often", so you will know quickly what you have to address.

Find the balance between intensity and relaxation in your mind. You'll soon start to realize how important and gratifying this moment really is.

The present moment may sound ordinary and boring. It's anything but. Being in this moment is not about controlling thoughts, it's being aware of them. Find the balance between intensity and relaxation in your mind. You'll soon start to realize how important and gratifying this moment really is.

Learning to be present can be one of the greatest things you do in your life because it will help you appreciate moments of beauty, moments of serenity and also just every-day moments that we too often take

21

for granted. The moment is where you are right now and what you're doing. How are you feeling? Thinking? Does this book consume you or are you thinking about the past or future? If you can become aware of this, you can then take the necessary steps to calm those thoughts of the past and future and focus your energy on the thoughts that will benefit you. Meditation can help you, but don't be put off by your initial attempts if you haven't meditated before.

> Our need always to be occupied means that being mindful takes the back seat. You have the ability to change that...

If you start to meditate, you'll notice how crazy some of the thoughts are that go through your head. You might even think you're a little crazy. I sure did. But these insane thoughts are normal, and learning to control them is also normal. Our western pace of life and our need always to be occupied means that being mindful takes the back seat. You have the ability to change that and it will only take a few minutes a day.

When meditating, try to focus solely on your breathing. Focusing on your breathing brings awareness to one thing and that is what being mindful is all about. When you start to meditate, your thoughts will slip and you'll notice yourself following some unwanted thoughts. When you become aware of this, you just refocus your thoughts on your breathing...in...out... Keep on repeating this to build strength of mind and also the ability to notice thoughts and correct them.

Time is an investment

Although the whole world revolves around time, is it not just an illusion? Is time a real thing? Is tomorrow a real thing? In our minds we are always thinking about today, tomorrow, yesterday, next month and next year. But we are rarely thinking about the here and now, this very moment.

After all, this very moment is the only moment we can control. This second is the only second we can be present in. We can't be present in next week, or the week after. The universe doesn't work like that.

Time is something that you can never get back, so why waste it in the past or the future? This doesn't make sense; get lost in the here and now.

I once heard our relationship with time explained in this way: Every morning when you wake up you are given $86,400 into your bank account, but at 12pm

23

each night, whatever money you haven't spent, invested or withdrawn, is taken away from you. What would you do? Take out every last cent, right? Each day consists of 86,400 seconds and those seconds are yours to invest, spend or just leave in your bank account to be wasted.

Choose what you want to do with your seconds, but choose wisely. Don't leave any money in that account. Don't waste any time.

Cycles

January happens every year, we all know that; it happened last year and chances are it will happen next year. But the difference is, the person you were in January of this year, you most certainly won't be that same person in January of next year.

Time moves on and cycles are not circles, you are not back to square one every January, or Monday for that matter. Think of cycles as a stretched-out slinky (something I will explain in more detail later on): when things don't go the way you wanted them to and you feel like your back to square one, you'll notice that you have in fact just gained a whole lot of experience, be that a day, a month or even a year. You'll also notice that you are acquiring the required skills for what the future holds. What you'll begin to understand is that everything you have thought or done in the past has got you to where you are right now in your life. Accepting this will bring you to a new level of clarity of mind, which is hard to find in modern society.

Learn in every moment to change every cycle.

I want you be able to stand back and say, "Wow, thank you, this moment is the only moment in my life right now."

When you were a kid, I bet you couldn't wait to grow up and become a teenager. And when a teenager, you couldn't wait to become an independent adult. Then in adulthood time seems to spin so fast and you begin to wonder where all those years have gone. All of these years you're constantly thinking about the future, looking forward to the next thing in your life that will bring "happiness". Well, happiness isn't a destination, it's a way of being. In saying this, I don't mean that happiness can't be found in an event or series of events, but what I am saying is that you need not rely on events to give you happiness, but rather create your own hap-

> "Time is a created thing. To say, 'I don't have time' is like saying 'I don't want to.'"
> — **Lao-Tzu**

25

piness within yourself. True happiness is to be found here, right now.

The wandering mind

A study by Harvard psychologists shows that about 47% of people's minds wander, and they concluded that a wandering mind was an unhappy mind. Humans are unlike most other animals as we spend a lot of time thinking about the past and future and are rarely focused on the here and now and the activity we are doing in this moment.

The psychologists developed an app that tested 2,250 people at random times of the day. The app got them to rate how happy they were and whether they were thinking about their current activity or about something else that was pleasant, neutral, or unpleasant. They could choose from twenty-two general activities, and the one that found them to be most focused was making love.

What the results showed was that the activity the person was doing only accounted for 4.6% of that person's happiness. This study teaches us that, regardless of circumstances, you can be happy, but ultimately, when you let your mind wander and don't try to settle your thoughts, this gives you a less happy mind.

Buddhism and some other religious and spiritual practices put a huge emphasis on meditation and being mindful. They believe that happiness is to be found in the here and now and not in the past or future (this isn't to say that you can't have happy memories). Mindfulness is a large part of being happy and focusing on one particular activity.

> Acknowledge the beauty of the world and how we have revolutionized and changed so many things.

Being present can be as simple as acknowledging where you are right now. Acknowledge the beauty of the world and how we have revolutionized and changed so many things. Beauty doesn't have to mean nature; beauty can be architecture, modern design and anything else for that matter. Even the simplest things have beauty in them. Acknowledge it and say thanks. Don't rush your most precious moments. Embrace them and live them, take it all in.

Take a snapshot

Take a snapshot of a moment each day. Be grateful for something — something simple that most people take for granted. When you do this, you'll realize how

27

much of life we take for granted when on autopilot. Do you remember the advert of Robbie Williams taking the picture of everyone taking pictures of him on stage? He was blown away with amazement. That can be you each and every day of your life if you can just appreciate the little things. Be blown away by simple things!

Why is this moment important?

This moment brings clarity to your thoughts and actions. Just appreciating right now can help you clear your head for a split second and just feel humbled. This moment is important because it allows you to experience life from a perspective unknown to most, a perspective of peace and clarity. This moment is important simply because it's the only place that you can physically be right now.

Being present will give you clarity of thought and appreciation of simple things, and this is a part of happiness

When you can learn to be in the moment, you can learn to appreciate things in a much clearer and simpler way. You might be curious about how right now can make you so "happy". I'm not guaranteeing that it will make you directly happy, but what I will say is that, with practice and persistence, being present will give you clarity of thought and appreciation of simple things, and this is a part of happiness. You'll soon realize that happiness is not one big event or circumstance but rather a series of thoughts.

How do I implement this into my everyday life?

You're probably thinking, "Hold on, all this talk about the moment and not a mention of how I'm actually going to implement it into my life." This little meditation exercise will help: Find a place to sit, preferably a quiet place. You might want to go where people can't see or interrupt you. Sit down and take a few deep breaths with your stomach moving slightly outwards when you inhale. Inhale...exhale...relax. Start from the tip of your head and work your way through your body, relaxing every tense fiber. Scan your body for tension. Close your eyes and bring all your attention to your other senses. What does the air smell like? What does the chair feel like that you're sitting on? What sounds do you hear? Gather all of this information and process it. You start to build a picture in your head of your surroundings and your awareness is heightened. You become aware of things around you, the sound of the birds or maybe the people walking by, or maybe the clock ticking. Some of these things

29

you might not be aware of when you are going about your day. Our pace of life is so crazy that it leaves little time for reflection. Becoming aware of your surroundings is being present. Do this exercise as often as possible. I can guarantee that very soon you'll start being mindful when doing other activities.

What you have done is become aware of your present surroundings. The reason I ask that you do this with your eyes closed is just to build a sensitivity and awareness for your other senses. You can do this exercise with your eyes open if you don't want to be noticed. Just become aware of your surroundings. Ten minutes of this a day will help you take a step back in life and just say, "Wow, thank you."

"Use your senses fully. Be where you are. Look around. Just look, don't interpret. See the light, shapes, colors, and textures. Be aware of the silent presence of each thing. Be aware of the space that allows everything to be. Listen to the sounds; don't judge them. Listen to the silence underneath the sounds. Touch something — anything — and feel and acknowledge its Being." — **Eckhart Tolle**

Time Perspectives

Living in the now is not possible all of the time, and there are naturally times when we need to deal with the past and with the future. It is a matter of having a good perspective on time. A good way to be is to focus on the positives of the past, be present as often as you can and focus on your goals in the future. This gives you a beautiful balance between the three. The present is all we can control, but you also need to learn from the past and work toward the future.

People who get so engrossed in the future and being successful sacrifice an awful lot in order to be successful. Sacrificing hobbies, downtime, family time and sleep, for example, can lead to burnout and lack of motivation.

I believe there is a time and place to sacrifice these things but don't get so extreme that you end up losing relationships and other important things. I think that being present is most important because when you get caught up in the future or the past, you are not doing what you can do right now to improve on the past or work on the future. Play with it and see what suits you...

LIFE INSIDE OUT

▶ Life is much better lived from the inside out.

▶ It means you choose how to feel, act and be.

▶ Get rid of your ego, it doesn't do you any favors.

▶ Be a tree.

▶ Build your foundation, and then build whatever else you want on top of that.

▶ Have awareness of your surroundings, but also of yourself.

▶ Self-awareness is the start of self-development.

▶ Give something back each and every day.

▶ You can live life inside out if you chose to do so.

Live life from the inside out

The title of this chapter might confuse you, but once you have read it, you will be blown away by how immune you can be to circumstance. Circumstances determine most people's feelings and attitude towards the world and towards other people. I'm here to tell you that you can let your attitude and feelings determine your circumstances. If you can change a few things, you can alter your perception of situations that you might once have thought to be negative.

Most people in the world are very much *out to in* people. Their circumstances affect their feelings and happiness. Being an *out to in* person is not good, because it means you have no control over the only thing in the world that you should and can control – your thoughts. Obviously we are not robots, so we can't feel great all day every day. But what we can do is try our best to be aware of our thoughts and of how things that we think are negative can actually be positive.

Ever hope or work for something and it doesn't work out and then you look back in a week, a month or a year and say, "Wow, I'm glad that didn't work out the way I wanted." Well, that's what this chapter is all about, not letting your circumstances control your thoughts and feelings. And by feelings I don't mean physical feelings, I mean mental and emotional.

In to out....

Being an *in to out* person just means that you are aware of situations and circumstances but you control how you react and perceive them, usually choosing to react in a positive manner. Being *in to out* is the best and easiest way to be happy. You may say, "But what if something happens to me and puts my life at risk, how can I be happy when I know I might die?" The answer is that you can still be happy. Obviously it is going to take more energy to be happy than if you had nothing wrong, but you can certainly choose to be happy. You can sit back and let whatever has happened take over your life or you can say, "No, I'm not going to let this determine how I feel, I'm going to have a blast until I beat this circumstance." See what you've done there? You have taken a devastating and clearly bad situation and turned it into something more positive. You are controlling all that you can control and you are channelling your energy in the right direction to enjoy yourself. Channelling your energy into better thoughts will help you see the world from a much better perspective. I know many people, some of whom

35

are friends, who always have something negative to say about everyone and everything; I too am guilty of this at times. And we all know how draining negativity like that can be. If, however, you can focus on the positives in the world and the positives in other people then you will bring out the positives in you. Yet again this is all down to self-talk.

When someone does something different, "out of the ordinary", people will sit up and take notice. But what is the ordinary? The ordinary is monotonous, boring and not a fulfilling life. Doing something different and great is fun and enjoyable and will make you energetic. What you do and how you do it is up to you. Create your own happiness, real happiness, from the inside out.

Out to in...

Out to in people tend to be very up and down in their emotions and feelings. Their circumstances rule their minds and their happiness. Its raining outside, so it's a bad day. No its not a bad day, it's a great day. You are alive, you woke up. You should feel blessed. What makes rain bad is that people tell you it is bad and you believe that it is bad. It can have bad effects on

the world, but ultimately that's to do with r
isn't anything you can control, so why '
worry about it? Negativity attracts negativity, ᴐᴗ
more negative you are, the more negative you and
your surroundings will become. I hate my job. Why?
You chose to hate your job. What about the millions
of people that are homeless and can't get a job? If you
hate your job, quit and do something
you like. Looking at the world with
a more open and in-tune mind will
make your days much better. Take a
leaf from this chapter and decide to
work on being an *in to out* person.
This means that you choose how to
feel, how to act and how to think. It will change your
life from the minute you start doing it.

> If you want to do something great with your life, you need to take risks and not be afraid to fail.

A little note on risk-taking. If you want to do something great with your life, you need to take risks and
not be afraid to fail. If you hate your job, why would
you stay there? You have to? Some circumstances will
mean you do have to stay in your job; if you do, why
not start working on something in your spare time?
Why don't you start taking night classes in that subject that you've always loved? If you aren't happy
with your current situation, one of two things has to

37

change: your perception of the situation or the situation itself. The decision is up to you. Go out there, take risks and do something great with your life.

E.G.O.

Dealing with my ego is where I have struggled a lot and still do sometimes. An ego can ruin everything you have. It can destroy relationships, yourself, your own happiness and all of your possessions. An ego is simply a false sense of yourself and the world around you. People with egos tend to be curt and sometimes rude, thinking the world revolves around them, and they also seem to think that anything bad that happens only happens to them.

"Attitude is everything, so choose a good one." This little affirmation is one that I learned from a guy called Wayne Dyre. I think it's an incredible affirmation, and it sums up "Life Inside Out". If you can choose the right attitude, you can be or become whoever and whatever you want to become. Get rid of your ego and treat others with the respect that you want to be treated with. Be loving, caring and anything else that is positive. After all, the vibes you give out to the world are the vibes that you will get back.

You may still be curious as to why being *in to out* can help you? If you're the type of person who says, "Well, I can't determine what happens to me, so why would I try to be happy when something bad happens?" Well, why wouldn't you try to be happy? Letting your circumstances determine how you see the world is the biggest reason so many people live a life of mediocrity. Most people work to survive, living just for the weekends, looking forward to Friday and dreading Monday. How can you ever be happy living like this?

The saying is very true that we become what we think. Everybody suffers from negative thoughts, emotions and circumstances; that's just life. But all this negativity doesn't have to determine your whole outlook on life.

> "Even after all this time, the sun never says to the earth, 'You owe me'. Look what happens with a love like that, it lights the whole sky." — **Hafiz**

Being *in to out* gives you the power and takes the power away from many circumstances. Life when lived this way is a beautiful place to be and it can allow you to experience everything from a more loving, forgiving and generous place. Becoming more loving, forgiving and generous has a ripple effect throughout your life. You will begin to see other circumstances through a different lens, and you will begin to be much more grateful. Being loving and caring is what we were always meant to be, but for a lot of us, somewhere in the years of growing up, our ego has taken over. This is not entirely your fault, as that is the way the world goes. I don't think it is true that the more things you have the more successful you are.

Having possessions can certainly be a sign of success, but success is a collaboration between many great things like hard work, giving back, gratitude, positivity and imagination. Learn to live life this way, and your world will change.

Be a tree

Think of yourself as a tree. A tree can stand small and sturdy but it can also be tall, strong and live for hundreds of years. A tree builds itself from the ground up and from the inside out. A tree is planted as a seed. That seed gets food, light and water — all it needs to live a fulfilled life. The seed then begins to grow and develop. Soon, after a year or two, there may be a small tree. But a lot has happened in that time. The tree's roots have grown out and down. They have formed a foundation, and as the tree grows bigger, so does its foundation. The tree will age, and with age comes maturity. The mature tree will have massive roots and may stand over a hundred feet tall. But the tree didn't get there overnight, and it most certainly didn't get there by just having its trunk planted in the ground. The tree got there because it followed its natural progression through life. It started as a seed and grew to be one of nature's most beautiful creations. Trees can withstand wind and rain, floods and nature, all because they have built themselves from the inside out.

> Living life from the inside out is simply stripping everything back, letting go of your ego and building a foundation.

A tree can also have branches and limbs cut off, but they will re-grow. A tree is constantly growing and reaching toward the sky. It can have good growth years and bad growth years, but it is always growing.

You too can be a tree. Even though you might not be in the frame of mind that you want to be in, you have time to improve on that. Living life from the inside out is simply stripping everything back, letting go of your ego and building a foundation. Life from the inside out means that you have the ability to continually grow, reach to become better and look at setbacks as opportunities to learn and improve.

As you progress and constantly learn, you are a successful person. Keep reaching towards the sun because, once you've reached out, you are already ahead of most people.

Mind, body, spirit

I believe we are three-part beings: mind, body, and spirit, and all three must be looked after.

Mind

I believe this is the most important part of us. Our minds determine everything that we do, say or experience. In order to look after the other two aspects of our life, I believe we first need to look after our mind. Our mind can be our most precious resource or our worst enemy. Looking after your mind is no easy task, but it most certainly is a task worth doing. Your mind will determine what your body looks like or feels like and your mind will also determine your spirituality. Your mind has the ability to make you into who you want to become. Give your mind the love and care it deserves, and live life from the inside out.

Body

I guess you've heard the saying, "Your health is your wealth". It is absolutely true, whether we mean our physical or mental health. In this instance we are talking about our physical health, but, again, good physical health starts in the mind with a decision to try and by looking at your physical health as a lifestyle and not as a chore. I believe each of these parts of our being feed into each other, and when you can gain mastery of one, you can gain mastery of the others that little bit easier. Getting yourself into good physical shape shows that you have the mental capacity to set a goal and work towards it. It's that simple. Look after your physical health like it's your child. Don't be so strict that your child feels controlled, but don't give your child too much room or it will go down the wrong path. Find a balance between enjoying yourself when you deserve it and being strict when you must be strict.

Spirit

The word spirit might lose a lot of people, and I don't want that. Spirituality to me is just being connected with the universe and has nothing to do with God, or Allah or any other supreme being. It is just about being in tune with the world and doing the things that

43

serve the world. It is being mindful and connected with other people and the world around you.

I believe that there is a law of attraction at work in the universe – that when you take one honest step toward your goal or toward doing something great, the uni-

You can attract anything you want into your life, and it starts by building a foundation.

verse works to help you. Doors will begin to open that you never even knew existed, and you will come in contact with people that you once looked up to. This to me is spirituality. Take honest steps toward doing something great and the universe will guide you along the path of least resistance toward your dreams.

This leads me into living from a place of awareness. Living from a place of awareness is a form of spirituality. You feel connected to something that you may or may not want to label. You can attract anything you want into your life, and it starts by building a foundation. Being aware that a new foundation needs to be built in order to get rid of the old one, or being aware that there wasn't a foundation there to begin with, is the first step to changing your life. If you can live your life from a state of awareness, you can begin to see things about yourself that need to be changed and you can also see things about yourself that are absolutely beautiful. Both are as important as each other. You must also be aware that your values govern your behavior. This means that whatever you value, you will behave according to that value. If you love socializing, you will work all week and live for the weekends. If you become immersed in work, you will see work wherever you go, constantly checking e-mails and rarely taking the time out to slow down and reflect. Whatever it is, being aware will be the initial step to changing anything you need or want to change. Live life from the inside out.

CIRCUMSTANCES AND EXPERIENCES

▶ You have the power to choose how circumstances influence your thinking.

▶ Choose to think of the positive in every situation, no matter what it is.

▶ You can change your circumstances and experiences by simply changing how you perceive them.

▶ Writing things down brings awareness.

▶ Be or become aware of how you talk to yourself and act on that awareness.

▶ Self-analysis helps you become very aware of why you are the way you are.

The power to choose

Circumstances have an enormous impact on your thinking, good and bad, but only if you let them. The cool thing, however, is that you have the power to choose how circumstances influence your thinking. Circumstances are what happen to you and experiences are how you perceive what happens. Take, for example, coming second to somebody in something. Those of you familiar with golf will remember Rory McIlroy's collapse on the back nine on Sunday in the 2011 Masters. A lot of people would have dealt with that as something negative and something bad, but in hindsight I believe it has had a huge part to play in Rory becoming the player he is today. That awful back nine would destroy anybody's confidence, but he didn't let it, and that's the difference. He took what seemed like a negative circumstance and turned it into a positive experience by taking everything he could from it — building on the good stuff and learning from the bad. Now Rory is back to the number one golfer in the world and certainly the most dominant player in the game today.

This story is a prime example of how you have control over your thoughts and how you react to any situation. Rory concentrated on the positives from the past, stayed in the present by focusing on what he could control every minute, and won the next major by a whopping eight shots and broke many records. He chose what to think and where to channel his energy, and it has worked with great effect.

> Choose to think of the positive in every situation no matter what it is. This is much easier said than done, but when it is done properly it can have incredible effects on your performance...

Choose to think of the positive in every situation, no matter what it is. This is much easier said than done, but when it is done properly it can have an incredible impact on your performance and future outcomes in sport, business or life in general. Being thankful in situations of distress or trouble can also help you see the brighter side of things. After all, stressful or troublesome situations give us the best chance to learn and grow. Live every moment.

Why do we see things the way we do?

We see things the way we see them simply because of our conditioning. We are brought up and usually live

49

the way our parents live. We learn from our parents, friends and family, although other people can also be massive influences. Many parents think that in order to create wealth and get a good job you must go to school, then university. The better the degree you get from a university, the more chance you have of getting a better-paid job. You then buy a house and pay into a pension so that you can retire happily. Although this way of thinking will surely get you through life, will it give you the financial freedom that you want? Will this way of thinking

> Surrounding yourself with the right people can play a huge role in changing the way you think, act and grow as a person.

help you LIVE or merely exist? The answer is up to you. If you ask yourself, "If I had all the money in the world, would I still do what I'm doing on a day-to-day basis?" You can then determine whether you are living or existing.

When we learn from our parents, friends, family and peers, we are more likely going to think, act and do the things that they do. This is why surrounding yourself with the right people can play a huge role in changing the way you think, act and grow as a person.

Learning from your parents doesn't mean that your

parents are going to sit you down one day and say, "Today we are going to learn about being happy." We learn by imitation, and doing what other people do.

Our conditioning comes from how we allow these people to influence us. I was very lucky to meet my golf coach, Seamus Duffy, when I was fifteen. Seamus has changed my life, instilling in me the importance of hard work and persistence but also the importance of self-analysis. I don't know if the self-analysis part was intentional, but I do know that he has had a huge impact on the way I look at life.

To change your life, you must first change your thinking. In order to achieve different results, you must do different things, and in order to do different things you must think different thoughts. You can change your circumstances and experiences by simply changing how you perceive them. In the next few pages we will talk about how to perceive situations from a different, more accepting frame of mind.

How do our perceptions affect our everyday lives?

Our perception, or how we view the world around us, can affect our everyday lives, because our perceptions form the lens through which we see life.

Your perceptions can change for better or worse, and learning how to change them for the better can help you become the person you want to become. If you see the world through a negative lens, then you will find the negative in everything that happens to you. You will not be able to accept the idea that a lot of things that happen to you are out of your control, and that no matter what you did, you couldn't influence how those events occurred. Have you ever found yourself in a traffic jam? You're furious. This has spoiled all of your plans and you're going to be late for your big meeting. Yes, this isn't a good situation no matter what way you look at it, but it is completely out of your control, so why let it bother you?

> If you see the world through a negative lens, then you will find the negative in everything that happens to you.

In this same situation, you can accept these circumstances as bad, but ultimately you can also accept that you had no control over them. Taking simple steps like this can change your perception of situations, and I believe this can have a domino effect throughout your life. Having a great outlook on one situation will bring you some awareness to how good it feels when you choose to be positive. The next time a negative situation occurs, you can choose to accept it and move on.

Gratitude can play a massive role on your whole outlook, and I would advise implementing as much gratitude into your life as possible. Just say thank you!

Activities

Anything you do during the day is a direct result of your self-talk. What you eat, what you do in work, at home and whether you work out or not. These all happen or don't happen because of that little conversation going on in your head.

It's crazy to think how much this conversation can influence your life experiences and what you do on a daily basis. I like to use mantras and affirmations to change my self-talk and I also like to write it down occasionally.

Writing things down brings awareness. Someone once told me, to think you must write, and I agree one hundred percent. I keep a journal and sometimes a self-talk journal, and both of these help me release some feelings and thoughts that I have throughout the day.

My journal also helps me build my self-belief because it allows me to focus on the positive things that I complete each day. We will discuss this valuable tool in a later chapter.

Be aware and act on it

Be or become aware of how you talk to yourself and act on that awareness. A lot of the time you will have to do the opposite of what your voice is telling you to do. I know from personal experience that I have to drag myself to the gym just because I have told myself repeatedly that it's okay not to go, and this is false. For my lifestyle choice, I need to work out and stay committed. It is a lifetime commitment to stay focused on working out and eating healthily. That's just a personal experience and it might not be the same for you, but if it is, take control of one thing at a time and it will cascade throughout your entire life. Becoming aware of self-talk will allow you to realize how you think and why you think the way you do.

Changing your self-talk

Self-talk can have a detrimental effect on how you perceive situations, and being able to manage your self-talk will allow you to manage how you think. Changing your self-talk involves firstly being aware and then talking to that little voice and telling it what you need to hear, not necessarily what you want to hear. Your untrained self-talk will always tell you what you want to hear and not what you need to hear, and this has a detrimental effect. Make a commitment to yourself to change your self-talk by first becoming aware of how you talk to yourself. If you don't want to change, that's okay too, but you will continually see the world the way you see it now, and if that's good enough for you then well done.

Routines and habits

I believe that routines and habits are all about self-talk. A habit or a routine is something that you do repeatedly. A habit is mostly looked upon as being a bad thing although a lot of habits are good. Habits all stem from self-talk, and if it starts from self-talk it can also stop from self-talk. Breaking a habit can be a lot of work but it can have huge effects on your psyche.

Routines are much the same as a habit. You do these repeatedly. For example, a top sports star might like to get to the track or playing field at least an hour before the game and go through the same stretching and warm-up routine every time they compete. I think that's great because it makes the athlete confident that

55

they are prepared. However, if the preparation hasn't been done months before, then the routine on the day of competition isn't going to make much of a difference.

Habits like smoking can also be broken. You can make a decision to stop, so don't give in now. Once you make that decision you are now strengthening your self-talk and your ability to be disciplined.

Routines and habits are a direct result of an initial self-talk and then repeating that self-talk. They then become nearly automatic and good routines build good habits. A habit is something like smoking, you do this repeatedly but you don't do it at a set time each and every day. Maybe some people do, but I would still look at smoking as a habit. A routine, however, is something like we already talked about. A sports star will have a daily routine and a tournament day routine. This is something that they do repeatedly without fail. Having a routine will help you get into a space mentally that a lot of your competitors can't get into.

If you can become aware of your habits and routines, you can begin to change the ones you don't like. If you can manage to build great habits, you will find it easier to build great routines. For example, if you were able to build in the habit of turning your cell phone off one hour before bed, chances are you will find it easier to get up earlier in the morning and change your routine of sleeping in.

Take an honest look at yourself and see what habits you can change, and when you have changed some habits, begin to build great routines.

Self-analysis

If you are a procrastinator, then chances are you'll always be a procrastinator until you become aware of it.

Self-analysis is similar to analyzing self-talk, but goes a bit deeper. Self-analysis helps you become very aware of why you are the way you are. More than likely, you are the way you are because of your conditioning. When you believe something, and you think something, you reinforce that thought in your being. If you are a procrastinator, then chances are you'll always be a procrastinator until you become aware of it and then act on it. People might tell you that you're a procrastinator, but until you realize it yourself and you are willing to change, other people's comments and advice are useless.

I believe that through self-analysis you can change

57

The snow globe

Imagine your mind as a snow globe. All day, every day, you are shaking the snow globe with the hope that the snow will suddenly settle to the bottom. But it doesn't, and you wonder why. Set the snow globe down, however, and suddenly, the snow settles and what is in the middle of the globe becomes clear. Your mind works in the exact same way. Unless you try to calm your mind, you will always have the snow globe effect going on. In the same way that the snow globe needs time to settle, so does your mind. You need to give your mind the correct nourishment to allow it to be calm and still and also to allow that picture to become clearer. Give your snow globe the chance to settle and reveal the beautiful image in the middle.

anything you want to change. You can change your mental or physical life. Being aware of your own self can be an extremely tough thing to do, but it can be your greatest asset. Money, cars, fame and everything else that is material can be taken away from you, but once you know something, you know it forever. With self-analysis comes a deeper understanding of yourself and your life. Self-analysis also helps you tap into your infinite imagination, providing you with some great insights and ideas for your life.

I find the best way to self-analyze is to sit down for ten minutes a day (minimum) and meditate. I meditate by focusing on my breathing. When meditating, I'm not trying to block out thoughts, or stop thinking, I'm simply becoming aware of thoughts and letting them pass. Doing this gives me a deeper understanding of myself, and I don't think you'll understand what I mean until you try it for yourself. Meditation is not a band-aid for the mind; it doesn't stop negative thinking for a short period. Meditation can be preventative and it can help you to stay focused, keep a healthy mind and also allow you to make choices that benefit you and your goals. Regular mindfulness meditation will allow you to take a step back from your thoughts and do nothing. This in itself will be a struggle for most people, and I certainly found it a struggle when I started, but what I have gained from it has definitely been worth that initial effort. I am now more aware, happy, creative and productive; and to me, this can only help me.

SUCCESS AS A WAY OF LIFE

▶ You have the ability to be successful.

▶ Success is more a state of being then a destination.

▶ When you succeed, many people will call you an overnight success. Laugh at them.

▶ Pick a role model and learn from them.

▶ We learn best by imitation.

▶ Each day, lay one brick as best as a brick can be laid.

▶ To beat procrastination, work in 20-25 minute sessions.

▶ You are a successful person the day you choose to put in the effort. Remember, you must do this most days.

▶ To be successful you must be willing to make sacrifices.

▶ Be concerned with your character and not your reputation; your reputation is only other people's perception of you.

"Success is peace of mind which is a direct result of self-satisfaction of knowing you did your best to become the best you are capable of becoming" — **John Wooden**, UCLA head basketball coach from 1948 to 1975.

What is success?

The way I like to think of success is as a state of being and a way of life. Success doesn't have to mean having millions of dollars, although that would also be welcome. Success comes from within. Success changes from person to person. One person might be happy owning a local shop and being able to support their family. Another person might not be happy until they own an empire, while yet another person might not be happy until they are living a minimalist lifestyle. Success is knowing that you did all you could in order to achieve your goals and aspirations. The houses, the local shop, the money, these are all by-products of you becoming the best you can be.

Success is not a destination, success is a state of being.

John Wooden is regarded as one of the best basketball coaches of all time. He led UCLA to ten NCAA national championships in a twelve-year span. What this man did was truly incredible. In interviews, John talked about the difference between winning and succeeding. He usually meant winning basketball games but what he said can relate to life.

The difference that I have found between winning and succeeding is that winning is a by-product of succeeding. If you succeed, you are doing the right things that benefit you and your goals, day in and day out whereas if you win, that is merely an outcome. Winning will happen more often when you succeed; work on yourself and don't be so caught up in results. If you can manage to look after yourself and what you do on a day-to-day basis, you are going to win in the near future. Outcome goals are great but the real goals that help you stay on track are the process goals. These are the little milestones you set yourself, the ones, if you put in the effort, you will achieve. If you can meet all of your process goals and give it your all, then you are a *successful* person —the outcome will happen.

> Outcome goals are great but the real goals that help you stay on track are the process goals.

John Wooden once said, "Never try to be better than

someone else. Always learn from other people and never cease from trying to be the best that you can be, after all, this is all you have control over. When you get too engrossed in the things that you have no control over it will adversely affect things of which you have control."

Be concerned with your character and nothing else. Work on it, improve it and change it...

Be concerned with your character and nothing else. Work on it, improve it and change it, but don't change it because of your reputation, change it because of you. Your character is your fingerprint. It is who you are.

Success and dedication

Have you noticed that anybody who is successful has never got there by accident? Nobody has ever been born a success. Holton Buggs once said, "It took me fifteen years to become an overnight success."

Dedication is something that a lot of us have, but only when we allow ourselves to access it. This means working hard enough to improve and make it to the top, but not so hard that you no longer want to do the thing you're doing.

Finding a balance between working hard and taking time off is the key to being able to stay dedicated for longer periods of time. Figure out what works for you and continually motivate yourself. By staying motivated, it is much easier to stay dedicated.

And while dedication to what you are doing is essential for achieving success, it is not the only essential ingredient. Many people spend thousands of hours working on the wrong things and, although they are dedicated, chances are they won't be successful because of how little they know.

As well as dedication and hard work, I put a big emphasis on knowledge and flexibility.

Knowledge is, well, knowing, or learning the skill that you want to acquire. In order to learn something, it is best to take it step by step after breaking it down into smaller parts.

It is important to understand, however, that learning a new skill and improving an existing one require different approaches. To learn a new skill, a skill that you haven't ever tried or are yet to master, that skill must be broken down into bite-size pieces. For example, children learning to read do not learn full words, they first learn the alphabet and the sounds that each letter makes.

However, when you want to improve an existing skill, it is important to make your practice as challenging as possible. There must be consequences to your practice, especially in sport. An example of this might be "Hell Week" when Navy SEALS are put through their paces. They are made to function with minimal sleep and always being wet, cold and tired. Why do they do this? They do this because when you know how to perform a skill, you then need to make that skill so instinctive that under pressure you can perform better than ever. A Navy SEAL's training is extremely tough and it prepares them for the battlefield.

To learn a new skill, break it down and make it simpler. To improve on an existing skill, make practice as tough as possible.

Flexibility is essential to learning and becoming successful because it allows you to adapt to new situations. The world is forever changing, and if you're not changing with it, you're falling behind. By flexibility, I don't mean physical flexibility, I mean flexibility of the mind and allowing yourself the space to improve.

To be successful you need to be willing to learn and to be flexible.

Bruce Lee once said, "*To be a great mixed martial artist you need to be formless, shapeless like water. Put water into a cup, it becomes the cup, put water into a teapot and it becomes the teapot, put water into a bottle and it becomes the bottle. Water can flow or water can crash. Be water my friend.*"

The message behind this is that you don't want to be so rigid in your thinking and your actions that you destroy your ability to improve. Don't be so set in your ways that you aren't willing to try something new. This isn't telling you to try every new idea out there, but if someone says something or gives you some advice, remember it, analyze it and then take what you want from it.

Don't be so set in your ways that you aren't willing to try something new.

Hank Haney, Tiger Woods' ex-coach, said that Tiger put in to play about ten per cent of what Hank taught him. Tiger had the ability to take information, process it, and then take what he believed to be relevant and use it. This is part of the reason for his golfing greatness. Being able to do this comes from experience, the experience of doing your own thing and seeing how it

67

works out. Did it work out if I did it the way my coach or my boss said? Yes? No? If so, why?

Becoming successful is not easy. It is a constant battle between what you want to do now and what you want to do or have in the future. The battle is in your head. "Should I go and do another hour of practice" or "should I watch my favorite TV show?" The choice is yours. If you have done everything that you have set yourself to do that day then yes, reward yourself. But if you haven't done everything you needed or wanted to do then no, go and practice or study. Don't reward yourself if you don't deserve it. When you do this it is much easier to do it again the next time. In order to become successful, just become the person you want to be. Work hard at it and put every fibre of your being into doing so; the self-satisfaction that comes will be something you might have never experienced before.

> In order to become successful, just become the person you want to be.

Role models

Most of us are not lucky enough to know somebody personally in our field of interest. But this doesn't mean that you can't learn from them. Imitation, which is how we mostly learn as children, is a great tool and can bring you a long way towards who you want to be. Pick your favorite person in your chosen field. Then go and research that person and maybe write an essay on their behaviors, work ethic and whatever other valuable nuggets of information that you can find about them. Some behaviors you'll want to stay away from and others you'll want to embrace.

After researching this person, try to imitate what they do. Do they get up early? Do they work out? How do they plan their day? You need to put your own twist on things, but using other people's ideas and creating the habits of highly successful people makes sense. We learn best this way, and it can be fun and challenging. Try to learn, study and imitate your hero. Maybe one day you'll be a hero to somebody else.

Beat that devil

That little devil called procrastination lurks everywhere. It comes up when you least expect it and it is always present. Procrastination is like a drug, it allows us to get immediately what we want immediately. This can sometimes be good, but while chasing a dream or pursuing a goal, it is bad.

69

Don't get me wrong, I don't expect you to be mechanical or robotic in your day-to-day life; after all you do need to enjoy life. But I do believe that if you want to achieve anything great, you must be willing to sacrifice some small things. You may have to sacrifice an hour in bed, or maybe a night out with your friends. Whatever it may be, it isn't anything that you can't do, and that's the reason you are going to be a success and some of your friends or peers won't.

To beat procrastination, you must first take away any temptation. If the temptation is not there, then you can't procrastinate. Taking away temptation just means that you don't need as much discipline to keep working on the task at hand. Although procrastination feels great at the time, it leaves us feeling down about ourselves and the more we do it, the more we allow ourselves to do it. It's a vicious circle and it's one to best stay out of.

How to concentrate

In order to work well, you need to have a clear mind and no distractions. No mobile phones, no nagging or screaming kids, and definitely no social networks. If you can work in 20-25 minute intervals with intense concentration and then reward yourself at the end of each 20-25 minutes with a small break, you will get much more done. Each hour, do this exercise, whether you're reading, writing, working, or practicing.

- ▶ 20-25 minutes intense, mindful work;
- ▶ 5-minute break. Reward yourself — even check Facebook, if you like, but have the discipline to leave your phone out of reach for the next 20-25 minutes;
- ▶ 20-25 minutes intense, mindful work;
- ▶ Repeat.

Lay one brick

To finish, I want to leave you with one of my favorite stories. As a kid, Will Smith's father tore down the wall outside of his store. The wall stood thirty feet long and sixteen feet high, with a six-foot foundation. He told Will and his brother to rebuild the wall, to which they replied, "That's impossible." The two boys came every day after school and after a year and a half had the wall rebuilt. Their father then said to them, "Now don't you ever tell me, there's something you can't do." As Will later said, this experience stayed with him. What he learnt was that each and every day you can lay one brick as perfectly as a brick can be laid — that he didn't set out to build a wall, but to lay a brick as perfectly

71

as he could, and the final result was a wall. The moral of this story is that each and every day for you is the equivalent of one brick, so lay it as perfectly as you can and you too will soon have something that you never thought was possible.

MANIFESTING INTENTIONS

▶ Before you achieve, you must believe.

▶ Write yourself something nice – a letter perhaps.

▶ A vision board will allow you to subconsciously manifest your intentions by constantly reminding yourself of what you want.

▶ Your intentions don't have to be 100% materialistic.

▶ Action is most important.

▶ You can't achieve greatness by just thinking about it, you must pursue it also.

▶ You choose your dreams and aspirations; don't let anybody else choose them for you.

▶ Your attention must equal your intention.

▶ FOCUS!

"You must begin to understand, therefore, that the present state of your bank account, your sales, your health, your social life, your position at work, etc., is nothing more than the physical manifestation of your previous thinking. If you sincerely wish to change or improve your results in the physical world, you must change your thoughts, and you must change them IMMEDIATELY." — **Bob Proctor**, *The Power To Have It All*

What is "manifesting your intentions"?

Manifesting your intentions is programming your mind to keep a sharp, steady focus on what you wish to achieve and thus train the subconscious to help you work towards those goals.

The most effective way to do this is by combining visualization with meditation. Visualization is simply having an absolutely clear and vivid vision of your objectives. If you are not completely certain that you have that vision, write a letter to yourself in which you include everything — physical, spiritual, and mental — you want in your life. This could include your dream home(s), car(s), food, clothes, vacation(s), money, love, family, loving partner, and every other little thing you can think of. This letter can be used as a reassurance that you already have what you aspire to have. Write this letter in the present tense to make it as realistic as possible.

I think it is best to put everything as if you have already got it because this reinforces your beliefs even further. "I love the new Ferrari I bought recently, the smell of the leather and the sound of the engine, and I want to thank you for helping me get this." I also believe that you need to have as much genuine gratitude in this letter as possible. Being grateful attracts more great things into your life. Don't think for one second that you are being selfish or greedy by wanting all these things, because if you can appreciate everything and work hard for it, you deserve everything that you've got. Go into the finest of details, explaining everything you have. This will give you a sense of realness and you'll be able to visualize it much more clearly.

Another tool I use to sharpen my visualization is a vision board. I have my vision board in my journal — a collage of pictures of my future goals. I also have the words "happiness" and "mindfulness" written large in my journal because I don't want to lose sight of what is most important to me. Combine that with the letter to yourself and you're well on your way to creating the foundations for your dreams.

Once you are able to clearly visualize what you want to achieve, it is important to start meditating on it. Meditating can be a bit of a pain for some people, and others simply think it's a daft idea. Trust me, it is great when you clear your mind and focus on one thing. Initially your mind will become more cluttered than ever, your thoughts will be everywhere except where you want them. Over time, however, your mind will begin to clear and you will gain control over your thoughts. The world will slow down, and this is a beautiful feeling.

When meditating, try and find somewhere quiet where you won't be interrupted for the duration of your meditation. Sit either on a comfortable chair with your feet flat on the floor, or on the ground with your legs crossed. Have a straight but not tight back and try to relax. Mindful meditation is my favorite because it helps me to focus on the thoughts I need to focus on and let the other thoughts pass me by. It's up to you how long you want to meditate for. I would recommend five to ten minutes per meditation to begin with, and you can build it up from there. Some people can meditate for hours on end. When you are meditating, just relax and try to focus on breathing in and out from your abdomen. When you have your breathing under control, you can then turn your focus onto whatever it is that you want to attract into your life. You can visualize yourself speaking in front of 10,000 people, or you can visualize yourself playing with the beautiful wife and kids that you want. Whatever it is, visualization

"Whether you think you can or you can't, you're right." — Henry Ford, founder of the Ford Motor Company.

meditation can help you achieve it. You are not trying to stop thoughts, or block them out. You are simply focusing on one thing (your intentions) and being aware of when your mind slips.

If your mind slips a hundred times, bring your attention back to where you want it a hundred times. Sit down and meditate, visualize what you want and attract that into your life. It is truly amazing. Meditation and life are very similar. In meditation, as in life, you will slip. You will make mistakes and follow the wrong thoughts or take the wrong actions. However, if you can be aware of your wrongdoings and focus on what you can improve on, you are going to be the person you want to be with a life full of promise.

Write down a few lines after you have meditated. This will give you clarity about what you saw and felt while you were meditating. By doing this you are tapping further into your subconscious and making yourself believe something that isn't true — at least, not yet.

What's the next step?

The next step is *action*. You need to understand how to get there, of course, but you need to take action immediately. We need to take action because thinking about it alone won't make it happen. In life we need a balance and in this situation we need a balance between what we intend to achieve and the action you take to achieve it.

There are a number of ways to help you take action, and in each of them you need focus. You need to be willing to focus for long periods of time in order to make your dreams a reality. There are two main types of initiation that I like to use to achieve optimal focus.

Conscious focus

This is simply choosing in your mind to be focused. You choose to have single-mindedness on the one thing that you want to accomplish. You are creating a practice to continually remind yourself to act in such a way that benefits your intentions. Mindfulness may help this. Mindfulness is just becoming aware of our thought patterns; when you do this, you can choose to channel your focus on your intentions.

Subconscious focus

A subconscious focus is where we create some type of subconscious response in the direction that continually moves us towards what we desire to create. Learning a habit or creating a belief and a way of thinking that reinforces action toward a desire will eventually sink into your subconscious. Ceremonies, cues and rituals are often used to create and then reinforce subconscious patterns that lead to action in a particular direction.

Conscious focus will eventually lead to a subconscious focus. As Robin Sharma, the author *The Monk who Sold His Ferrari,* has explained, your subconscious controls about 90% of what you do, and your conscious mind controls about 10%, but your subconscious is 100%

79

of what your conscious mind has told it in the past. So focus on your thoughts and your subconscious will look after itself.

It is also important to realize that your attention must equal your intention. If you have an intention to win an Olympic gold medal, then the attention that's required to do this is incredible. You can't intend to win a gold medal in the Olympics and then train once a week and expect to achieve. It doesn't work like this. Dreams don't work unless you do. So before you set your intentions, take a step back and think, "can I and will I give this enough attention to make my dreams become a reality"? If you answer yes, truthfully, to both of these questions then you're well on your way. Set your intentions high, but make your attention higher.

If you had only one hour a day to work on your dreams, what would you do for that hour?

I want you to be able to approach every day with the idea ; "*if I only had one hour a day to work on my dreams, what would I do for that hour? How would I plan that hour and what would be the most effective ways for me to get things done*"? If you can approach your day with this mindset, there is no reason why you should fail.

The Slinky Effect

The slinky effect is a great way to help you change your outlook to a more positive state. It is something I learned from a guy who helped me with my golf game, but I now realize it can be applied to life in general.

Imagine a slinky stretched out along a table, it's like a series of circles but they keep going, circles that are joined together and are always moving forward. Think of this as your life.

Have you ever worked hard at something and then have everything go off track so that you think you have made no progress and are back where you started? Well you are not. Why? Because you are never back to where you started. You have just gained a day, month, or year of experience in trying to accomplish the task that you set out to accomplish.

So don't think that you have just done a full circle and you are back to where you started, think as though you have completed a full circle in the slinky and you are much further past where you started. This is life; it never stands still and never goes backwards. The next time you go off track or have a blip in your plan and feel as though you're back to where you started, just remember, life is a slinky and you're way ahead of where you were when you started the task at hand.

Recently I had a bad year on the golf course. Instead of dwelling on the negative aspects of this, however, I put it down as a learning experience and re-assessed my strengths and weaknesses and how and where I went wrong. This has given me a lot of things to build on and work towards.

A lot of people assumed that I felt very disappointed, but in fact I am happy with how the year went, for many reasons — I handled myself well, I worked extremely hard and I gained a lot of experience. After all, the definition of success that I use is John Wooden's:

"Success is peace of mind which is a direct result of the self-satisfaction of knowing you did your best to become the best you are capable of becoming".

I believe I had a very successful year and I know that in the future, good results will be a by-product of all the work that I do.

STAYING MOTIVATED

▶ Motivation is like many good things in life, it doesn't last.

▶ To stay motivated, you must first be interested.

▶ Find your end goal and work backwards.

▶ Stay motivated by continually telling yourself what you want and why you want it.

▶ Motivation is not a destination; it is something that must be repeated daily.

▶ The easiest way to stay motivated is to enjoy what you do.

▶ Stay hungry.

Developing the motivation skill

Motivation is like so many other good things in life — it doesn't last. You need to continuously motivate yourself in order to stay interested in the task you are trying to complete.

Motivation can be intrinsic or extrinsic and each can have a hugely different impact on your day-to-day feelings. Intrinsic motivation comes from within and extrinsic motivation comes from outside sources like friends, coaches, family or peers. A balance of the two can be great, but in my opinion the more important motivation is intrinsic for the simple reason that it is more sustainable.

The ability to stay motivated is a skill and is best developed in tough times. To use sport as an example, it's easy to work hard when things are going well, but it isn't so easy to work hard when you feel as though you are struggling. Likewise, its easy to get up at 5am and go to practice when the sun is shining and you have a tournament in two weeks, but how easy is it to get out of bed in the middle of winter when its still dark at 5am and your next tournament isn't for six months? The answer is that it can be just as easy as long as you channel your energy in the correct way. Intrinsic motivation is a form of self-talk and it is basically convincing yourself that you want to do something even when you could think of a hundred things you'd prefer to do at that particular moment. Sometimes it can be as simple as just going and doing it and not thinking about anything else, working off intuition and not intellect.

Extrinsic motivation is different and is tougher to keep up for long periods of time, unless you have a full time coach-mentor to keep you in tune. Extrinsic motivation can be inspiring. Listening to stories about successful people in your field or seeing someone succeed in your field can be a great way of extrinsically motivating yourself. Some people find this more beneficial to them, but it isn't something you can rely on because it is an outside source of motivation. The saying goes, if you want something done, do it yourself. Motivate yourself from within. Combining intrinsic and extrinsic motivation can make your work ethic soar.

> Combining intrinsic and extrinsic motivation can make your work ethic soar.

I believe that motivating yourself from within and then taking advantage of any stories, videos or experiences that you may come across is the best way to stay motivated and hungry. So how do you motivate your-self? Well, first you need to have something to work towards: an end goal. From that end goal work back-wards. You want to get all A's in your end of year ex-ams? Ask yourself these questions. "What other exams do I have between now and then"? "What class tests have I got coming up?" When you know these things you can then just plan around them. I know I have a class exam in two weeks, so what can I do tomorrow to prepare for that exam? Set yourself goals for each day, things you want to get done. Process goals. Lit-tle by little, doing the correct things on a daily basis for a whole year, you'll be amazed at your results. Pro-cess goals are very important because they give you a specific set of tasks to do each day. A process goal will look something like this: study for two hours to-morrow on algebra, Chapter Two. It's simple, but not many people can do it. This will then lead you to your end goal, which will be getting an A in math. If your results don't work out the way you intended, then we will see who is motivated and who is not...

Use any sources possible to stay motivated and, as Mi-chael Jordan has said, keep adding logs to that fire.

Stay hungry and stay humble.

How and why?

Let's look at some ways that motivation can benefit you and your goals. As I have already pointed out, motivation of any type doesn't last forever. You have to continually motivate yourself. Motivation will benefit you and your ability to get things done, simply because that is what drives you or gives you the inspiration to do what you want to do. When you are motivated from within, you will start to be more meticulous and less carefree. You will work harder and hopefully smarter.

To find out what way you are motivated, ask yourself this series of questions:

▶ What motivates me? Is it cars, money, fame, ego?
▶ Is it a sense of accomplishment, self-fulfillment and improvement or self-improvement? Or is it a combination of a few of each?
▶ Why does this motivate me?
▶ What will I do when I reach my goal?
▶ How will I stay motivated in the future?
▶ What motivation do I prefer? Videos, stories, etc. Or do I prefer to visualize myself at a particular point in my life?

If you can figure out the answers to these questions,

you can then go about setting some ideas and goals that will motivate you in the way that you like. If you are a person who wants to accomplish something simply for reasons of money, fame and an ego, what do you do when you reach your goals? What will motivate you when you have fame and money? Figuring these things out will help you to enjoy the process much more.

I don't disagree with wanting to be famous, having cars and money, or having a dream home. That's what I certainly want, but what is more important to me is finding happiness in doing what I love to do, enjoying the process. I believe that you need to have a balance between material goals and personal, self-fulfillment goals. Find out what drives you. What gets you out of bed in the morning? If it is too much of one thing, then change that.

If you can enjoy the process, the end result will be much sweeter.

Try and set yourself some goals that will help keep you motivated continuously. Take a sales person for a company. Lets say that James earns $200,000 annually but he is on 5% commission for sales under $1,000,000 per year and with anything over that he receives 10%

commission. James is an extremely hard worker and he wants to be able to retire at forty. What motivates him? Well...a few things:

- ▶ the money he can earn;
- ▶ the idea of retiring at 40; and
- ▶ the amazing 10% commission on all his sales over $1,000,000.

This is what gets James out of bed in the mornings. James has the option to work extremely hard now and for the next few years but then retire at forty, or he has the option to slowly drift along, earn a good living and maybe retire at fifty-five. If you were James, what would you do?

I use this as an example so that you can see one thing: James reaches his first goal but then he has another goal waiting for him, another reason to work even harder. This is why I believe that it is important to have a balance between process and outcome goals when extrinsically and intrinsically motivating your-self.

ROCK BOTTOM AND BACK

THE KEY POINTS

▶ You can hit rock bottom, but you can also make it back to the top.

▶ If you fail once, don't give up. Try, try and try again.

▶ Nothing will happen until the time is right.

▶ Work hard and allow everything to fall into place; the only thing you can control is you.

▶ Through persistence and perseverance, anything is possible.

▶ You are unique. Be you.

My best friend's story

I would like to share my best friend's life story with you. Having had a tough upbringing and failing at school, he was on a road to nowhere worth going. He rarely went to school and started drinking and smoking cigarettes when he was ten.

We spent a lot of time together when I was in my mid-teens. We spent hours discussing life in general, often while watching our shared passion — the PGA golf tour. I think these few years might have planted the seeds of my willingness to learn and study. After hours of talking and discussing some things that maybe a sixteen-year old shouldn't know about his best friend, we developed a strong bond and fed off each other.

By eighteen he had a drinking problem. In his early twenties he moved to New York City. He went on a two-week holiday but never intended to come home. What better place to be in the world if you're an alcoholic? He worked in many bars in his six years in New York, and that was the dream: sex, drugs and free alcohol, even when working. It was like being a kid in a candy store. His lifestyle consisted of getting up about 11 am, eating breakfast and opening his first can of beer , starting work between 5pm and 7pm, already drunk, and working until the bar closed at about 5am. This went on for six years before it really took a big toll on his health.

When he moved back to Ireland he weighed about 135 pounds — clearly underweight for a six-footer. Being at home didn't put an end to the partying. It continued for many years despite the efforts of his mother and many other close friends and family to get him to realize that he was powerless over alcohol. After another few hospital visits and once having to call an ambulance to go to Emergency, it was time for him to give up alcohol. He attended meetings of Alcoholics Anonymous (AA) for a few months and was clean from drink, but then the wrong type of self-talk kicked in, and he convinced himself that he was able to drink at the weekends. This was never going to end well because alcoholism is a disease that you are powerless over, and until you accept that, your chances of recovering from it are practically nil. The drinking continued, spilling back into the rest of the week, for another six months — and this was what he calls the worst six months of his life, having to drink a liter of vodka in the morning before work just to stop his hands shaking. Can you even comprehend that?

After more talking and convincing and a little time in rehab, he went back to AA and this time there was a better outcome. That was in 2006, and to this day he has not touched a drop of alcohol. I'm not going to say, and he wouldn't say it either, that he will never touch alcohol again, but what he has done (to the best of his ability) is to take each moment as it comes. This may also be tough to comprehend, living each day in the moment, but if his mind slips and he starts to think about the future then he is opening himself up to a thought pattern that might hinder him staying sober.

The road to recovery has been long and hard but he has persevered. It hasn't been without its ups and downs but it has been a road to becoming an incredible person. This is not to say that he has never been an incredible person, but that beautiful person was masked by alcoholism and drug addiction. A fire burns strong inside him, a fire of self-worth, curiosity and love for the main woman in his life, his mother. Without his mother I don't think he would ever have become sober. She has been the most influential and inspirational person for him because she never gave up hope but prayed and prayed, and her prayers have been answered. None of us ever know what the next minute holds in store for us, but what we can do is take every second of life and cherish it. Embrace the challenges of life and know that, no matter what happens, we can overcome any obstacle. To me, he was and still is a big reason for me diving into self-study and trying to understand the way I think. I'm very proud of him and I wish him many more years of sobriety.

Keep it in the present and be happy to be alive.

There is a great lesson in my friend's story. Remember to live life in the moment you are in whenever possible and also remember that no matter what life throws at you, you can overcome it. Staying sober is a full time job and you can't let your mind slip. Awareness is the key to being able to correct your thoughts, and this is a constant battle for anyone, especially recovering addicts of all kinds. Keep it in the present and be happy to be alive. If I can get one point across to you from this chapter, it is that you can hit rock bottom, you can be broke, you can have many addictions but you can overcome almost anything. You've got to find the courage inside yourself to pick yourself up, dust yourself off and keep going. It will not, let me repeat, *not* be easy but any place worth going is not going to be easy.

INCREASE YOUR PRODUCTIVITY

▶ You can be greatly productive.

▶ Productivity and discipline go hand in hand.

▶ Have a basic plan for each day – it can go a long way.

▶ Prioritize!!

▶ Record your social media, cell phone or TV usage.

▶ Get rid of any distractions when trying to focus.

▶ Mindful work is the key.

▶ Write in your journal – keep track of each and every day.

▶ Be a minimalist for a week and see how it goes.

How to get things done

Productivity is the ability to get things done, and self-talk has an important role to play in how productive people are. Self-talk determines whether you decide to work on your goals or whether you procrastinate. Efficiency and productivity go hand in hand. When combined, they can be an incredibly powerful tool and an accelerant to success.

In order to become more productive, we must have a basic plan for our day. Previously I talked about the importance of living in the present and now I am talking about putting plans in place for the future, which may seem contradictory but in reality it is not because planning for the future does not mean living in the future.

Obviously we can't plan for what life throws at us, but what we can do is set out a template of what we want to do and when we want to do it. Have an idea of what you want to do and when you want to do it, and then live with the flow. Living with the flow is living with the understanding that "some things will happen to me that I have no control over."

To the unproductive person, a schedule can be daunting. It can work the wrong way and end up making one more unproductive. To counteract this, set some basic things you want to get done the following day. When you become more productive you can start to put more detailed schedules in place. Walk before you run. Don't overwhelm yourself with twenty things that you must get done tomorrow and then realize that you left no time to eat or reflect.

If you can set aside ten minutes every evening and plan your next day, you are already way ahead of most people.

Another great addition to every day, no matter how productive you are, is to write down three of the most important things you need to get done the following day. This gives you a few small things to do but isn't too overwhelming.

If you write a schedule or a to-do list for the following day, it doesn't need to be so rigid that you can't alter it. It needs to be rigid enough, however, for you to do what needs to be done. When creating a schedule, whether you're a businessperson, a sports person or just somebody who is looking to be more productive, use the *WIN* formula.

WIN — what's important now?

Ask yourself this question when creating your schedule or to-do list. When you can prioritize what is important, then you can get the right things done. In saying this, there are going to be tasks that you don't like doing or don't want to do, but if these are the more important tasks or practice drills then you *must* get these done first. Why? Not only will this help your mental state throughout the day, it will also help you get more done. If you have a task to do like laundry, and you dislike laundry but it needs to be done, then get up in the morning and do your laundry first thing. Prioritize it so that you no longer have to think or dwell on this. Being productive in this way will also help you to stay in the present because it will take your mind away from the activities you don't like to do and you can focus your attention on right now.

TV, cell phones and social networks

I don't watch a lot of TV and I don't have social networks on my phone but I still spend far too much time on my cell phone. Why? Habit. Productivity is all about breaking bad habits. A study has shown that the average American spends about thirty-four to forty hours a week watching TV. That's a full time job for some people. That's 76.5 days per year, which means that every 4.5 years the average American has spent one full year watching TV.

That's a lot of time — a lot of that time that could be spent doing other, more productive things. Don't get me wrong, watching TV can be relaxing, and downtime is also a big part of being productive because it can help you recover and get your mind away from the craziness of everyday life. Mental burnout can affect productivity just as much as a bad mindset. To

> Cell phone and social networks kill productivity completely. They are addictions in our lives...

my mind, an average of an hour a day is plenty of time for TV. Next time you go to watch TV, ask yourself, have I done everything that I set out to do today? If you can answer yes, truthfully, then go and enjoy yourself.

Cell phones and social networks kill productivity completely. They are addictions in our lives and they are so "important" in society that a lot of people couldn't survive without them (or at least they think they couldn't). Next time you're walking around a city or on a train or on any kind of public transport, have a look around and just observe the amount of people on their cell phones. It may help you understand how much time you yourself waste on your cell phone.

Social networks are anything but social, they kill productivity and the ability of people to interact with each other. Don't get me wrong; they are great for keeping in touch with friends and family worldwide, but all in moderation. Next time you check your phone or go on a social network, keep a note of it (on your phone) and you'll be blown away by the amount of times you check your phone or check your social network. Become conscious of your time spent doing unimportant things and then do something about it.

This brings me back to awareness: being aware of your use of social media is the first step to being able to control it and ultimately change bad habits. Maybe give yourself ten minutes to an hour a day where you can check Facebook or Twitter; apart from that, try to stay away from them. I found myself checking them about thirty times per day, so I deleted all apps off my phone that could affect my productivity. Deleting Snapchat, Instagram, Twitter and Facebook has led to a significant improvement in my ability to get things done.

Minimalism

Minimalism is taking something or many things out

of your life for a period of time. It means living without a lot of possessions. Why not take something out of your life for one month and see how you get on without it. Did your life benefit without this possession or were you unable to cope? If you couldn't cope, then put this one thing back into your life, but try putting it back to a lesser degree. For example, take away your mobile phone for the majority of the day. How was it? Did you enjoy it? Were you freer? How did it make you feel? Ask yourself these questions and you'll know whether or not this "thing" is benefiting your life.

Adding productivity to your everyday life

Productivity is a skill that can definitely be learned. To help you with this, and to put into practice everything you have learned from this book, I have designed a companion journal/diary. The journal combines many aspects of your life into one, simple to keep space. It has areas for magnificent statements, areas for affirmations, gratitude, daily schedules, daily priorities and goals.

This journal is very self-explanatory and the first few

pages give you a sample week. You can also record thoughts, feelings and emotions each day. It contains a weekly review where you can put what was good, what was bad and what can you improve on. This journal will give you the organization and structure that you need in order to reach any goals or dreams that you may have.

"Writing in a journal reminds you of your goals and of your learning in life. It offers a place where you can hold a deliberate, thoughtful conversation with yourself."— **Robin Sharma,** *The Monk Who Sold His Ferrari*

We will look in more detail at the benefits of keeping a journal in the chapter titled "Doing it the write way". One of the great advantages of keeping a journal is that it allows you to clear away any garbage that is in your mind and concentrate on what is important. It will also help bring structure and balance to your life.

I believe that keeping a journal will result in your life being profoundly different after a year. If you could get rid of negative thoughts each morning, plan each day and set goals for every week, don't you think that one year from now your life could be dramatically different and better? If you could take thirty minutes each day to record in your journal, you will be miles ahead of anybody else who isn't doing it. You might not want to keep everything in one journal. You may want one journal for schedules, to do lists, priorities and meetings while also having another journal for thoughts, feelings and emotions. You may even want to use your notes in your cell phone for gratitude. Where you decide to record all of this is irrelevant, actually recording it is the important thing.

All that I have done with the journal I have designed is allow people to record all of this in one simple, clean and easy to use space.

MEASURING YOUR PROGRESS

▶ Progress can be tracked.

▶ As long as you are doing the correct things, you are progressing.

▶ Don't look for instant gratification. It is counter-productive to progress.

▶ Although it may seem like you're getting nowhere, you are always moving forward.

▶ Even the greats have struggled.

▶ Invest in yourself, it's extremely fulfilling.

▶ Every honest step you take toward your goal is much more than the person who isn't taking any.

▶ Enjoy the ride, that's the fun part.

▶ Even the greats have struggled — Yes, I did repeat myself.

Be SMART

You want to achieve something important in your life and are putting in the effort and commitment day by day to work towards your dream. Sometimes, however, it can be hard to see if you are in fact making any progress, especially when you get better at something and any improvements come in small, and not too obvious, measures. Therefore, in order to keep your motivation as strong as ever it is important that you break your overall goal into a number of smaller goals that will act like milestones on the road towards your final destination.

These goals need to be SMART — specific, measurable, achievable, realistic, and time-targets.

Specific

This means that your goals must be very focused and broken down into smaller, bite-size pieces. Instead of saying I want to lose twenty-eight pounds in the next fourteen weeks, why not break that down and say, I want to lose two pounds this week, and continue to try and replicate that every week for the following thirteen weeks.

This way of breaking down a goal makes it, firstly,

much more attainable and, secondly, increases motivation because it is a short-term goal and you are not so focused on a time that seems a lifetime away.

Measurable

There are two ways in which a goal can be measurable: you can measure the outcome or the process. Using the example from above, the outcome is simply measured by the weighing scales to see if you have met your target of two pounds this week.

Measuring the process involves recording and analyzing what I did to reach that goal. Did I eat only organic foods, for instance, or did I allow some junk food to sneak into my diet? What amount of training did I do today and was it sufficient?

Being able to measure the process is important. If you eat perfectly and train hard for a week and don't lose the weight, does that mean you failed because you didn't meet your goal? In my eyes, no. Why? Because you did all you could do, and the results didn't go your way. My measure of success is partly results and mostly effort. I believe effort is the true test of character. Make you goals measurable and make them process-orientated.

Achievable

Achievable goals can also be process or outcome. Achievable process goals are obviously, well, more achievable, but a balance between achievable process and outcome goals can be a great recipe for success. An unachievable goal can make you unmotivated and it works this way because it seems that little bit too far out of reach. This isn't saying, don't dream; just don't expect to lose all twenty-eight pounds in the first week.

Realistic

This is similar to having achievable goals. Realistic goals are goals that are in reach but are hard to achieve. A goal like this for me might be, win an Irish amateur golf championship in 2015. In my mind, this is a realistic goal and it is most definitely within reach for me, but it is just far enough away for me to have to work my ass off.

Time

Setting time targets is important for productivity and getting things done, but you still have to be careful how you approach this. I think it is wrong to say, for instance, that by April 22, 2015, you will have lost fifty pounds. What you can say is that by April 22, 2015, I will have fully committed myself to my goals. That's all you can do. I don't think you can predict precisely how your own body will react to certain actions. I believe all you can control is what you do, and when the time is right, provided you have done the work, then the results will begin to appear.

Instant gratification

Instant gratification is something that a lot of undisciplined people suffer from, including myself. Instant gratification is like a drug but it only lasts a matter of seconds and then you realize, I shouldn't have done that.

If you can defer instant gratification, your productivity levels will soar while your procrastination will be swallowed up by endless work. In simple terms, instant gratification is sitting two kids down and saying you can have one sweet now or, if you wait thirty minutes, you can have two sweets. The kid that waits is the kid who can defer instant gratification.

This is a tough subject because we as human beings love instant gratification. We want things now and don't think of waiting a little longer to get better results. Ever been working and realize that you've just

111

wasted half an hour on the Internet? This is a type of instant gratification: you are looking for something to please you at this very moment. I have most certainly found myself doing this, not the working part, but the gratification part.

Delay gratification, stay focused and stay hungry.

Learning

When you're on a quest to achieve a goal, you learn. You learn things about yourself, your thoughts, your actions and your emotions. Writing down how you feel and how your day went is a great way to learn. I'm a big believer in keeping a diary, and it's not just about keeping track of things. Imagine you're doing well at something, be it a sport, business or just life, doing what you've planned to do each day and getting things done. By writing every night how your day went, how you felt and acted and what influenced your actions, you are laying down a way of learning about how to get yourself back into that good frame of mind at a later stage. Analyzing your day-to-day actions is important, of course, but it is also essential to find a balance and just at times let everything flow. This is something I need to remind myself about.

I don't believe you can force things. You can work as hard as you want but you've just got to let things happen. Learning to do this can be a bit of a pain — learning that maybe this year isn't the year that I'll make it as a professional golfer, but if I continue to work as hard as I do, someday it will all pay off. Learn to live life to the full, analyze a little and live a lot — and by living I mean being present in the now, as this is the only moment you can control. Learn to be grateful for things that may even seem silly, and learn to learn.

Even the best have struggled

The most disheartening feeling on the road to any destination in life is that feeling of getting nowhere, like you're at a standstill or even moving backwards. The good news is, you're not, and you never are. And neither are you alone in feeling that way. Even the best have struggled at one point. Let's look at a few examples:

Walt Disney

Despite his huge success in setting up a company that is now worth billions, Walt Disney didn't make his fortune that easily and was fired by a newspaper editor because "he lacked imagination and had no good

113

ideas." Then he started Disney but again not with much success as this venture ended in bankruptcy.

After years of hard work and persistence, however, it all paid off and Disney is the empire that we know it today. What Walt Disney did was nothing short of extraordinary, and his recipe for success, apart from great imagination and creativity, was hard work and persistence.

Albert Einstein

When you think of Albert Einstein, what do you think of? Genius? Well in my eyes, he was. But he sure as hell wasn't born this way. Einstein didn't speak until he was four and didn't read until he was seven and when he attended school his teachers thought he was mentally challenged. They couldn't have been more wrong.

Eventually after Einstein was expelled from school and refused admission into college in Zurich, the future didn't look bright for this "mentally challenged" kid. It might have taken him a little longer to learn, but it was worth the wait, as he went on to win a Nobel Prize and also changed how we see physics today.

Michael Jordan

Many people think that Michael Jordan has been a superstar all his life. But a childhood prodigy he wasn't. Jordan was cut from his high school basketball team, and it was said that he would not be anything special. If you ever watch Jordan's Hall of Fame acceptance speech, you can feel the belief he has in himself. The reason he says he succeeded is because he failed so many times. He talks about some setbacks and how players, coaches and friends challenged him in different ways, and all these challenges were like putting another log on an already blazing fire. Michael Jordan was hungry for success. His famous saying is, "I have missed more than 9,000 shots in my career. I have lost almost 300 games. On twenty-six occasions I have been entrusted to take the game winning shot, and I missed. I have failed over and over and over again in my life. And that's why I succeed." All these failures kept putting logs on the fire and kept Michael Jordan working hard and staying hungry. This is part of the reason why he is the greatest basketball player of all time.

The message I am trying to get across to you here is that although it may seem that you are not progressing at what you're trying to accomplish, you are. You are always getting better at something if you know how to go about what you're looking to achieve. This is why it is important to record your thoughts, feelings, emotions and actions.

Recording these will help solve the puzzle of the ongoing battle in your head. Again, this relates to the slinky effect. If you are not progressing, but time is still ticking, are you really in the same place? Progress doesn't always have to be as clear as day, it just has to exist, and with hard work it always exists.

Investing in yourself

A great lesson I learned from a family member was how to invest in myself.

I have been interested in investing in financial markets since I was fifteen so I decided one evening to call my dad's cousin in New York, an extremely intelligent guy who works as an engineer for a large multinational. He is also clever with his money, and I was aware of that, so I said I'd call him and see what he had to say. I had some money and I wanted to invest in the financial markets.

After a while, just talking, asking the usual stuff, he

said, "So you want to invest?" I said yes, hoping for some great formula or some great cheap stocks that would earn me a fortune, but what he said to me was, "All the money that you have now is only a tiny fraction of what you will have in the future, so investing now won't make a huge difference to your future anyway, although it might be a great way to learn." I thought, God, this is a waste of time, but what he said next hit home. He said, "Invest in yourself." Simple, invest in yourself and invest in what you want to do and the money will look after itself. I think this little lesson is a great lesson for anybody who is looking to become more successful or just happier: invest in you.

> "If today were the last day of your life, would you want to do what you are about to do today?" — **Steve Jobs**, founder of Apple

You might ask, well how can I do that? Easy. Find what you love to do and work hard at that; this is investing in yourself. Investing in yourself can be one of the most incredible feelings you will ever experience — fulfillment. In my journey, I have found that investing properly in myself gives me a sense of being and it makes me feel as though I am doing something with my life.

117

What are you doing for yourself?

Are you really investing in yourself and your dreams? Or are you investing in your parents' or peers' dreams for you? I have been very lucky to have parents that have never directed me in any one way. Yes, they have tried to get me to go to college but they have never made me do anything against my will, except go to school, and I believe that this can have a huge impact on what you decide to do. Ask yourself, why are you doing what your doing? Is it for you, or for somebody else? By asking yourself this, you'll soon realize if you're doing what you want to do with your life. This isn't to say that you shouldn't do things for other people, because helping other people is another great way of showing gratitude. I'm talking about your career when I say to ask yourself, "Am I doing what I want to do"? When you find out what you want to do and you start to work at it, you'll soon realize if this is what you really want to do, and when you're working on what you love, you'll find a deep sense of self-fulfillment. This is finding your inner legend and it's what Paolo Coelho talks about in *The Alchemist* — a must read for anyone who is interested in finding out what they want to do with their life.

Recovery is key, rest is overrated

There is an important difference between rest and re-covery. Recovery is what all the top athletes do. They work out, they train, and then they recover and do it all again. Rest is what lazy people do. This is the difference. There is definitely a time and place for resting and doing what you want to do, but mostly it is just recovery that is needed.

Recovery is rest in a way, but it's focused rest — focused on getting yourself back to top shape so you can go and train again or go back to work early tomorrow morning. Many athletes takes naps during the day. This isn't being lazy, this is getting their bodies back in shape for their afternoon session. This book isn't aimed at athletes in particular, but I think they are a good example. Many of them have their meals already prepped, their physio appointments booked and their training gear ready for their afternoon session. Once their morning session is complete, the focus turns like a light switch from training mode into recovery mode — getting the right nutrients into themselves and the right amount of everything to help their muscles recover and get to their optimum energy levels for the afternoon.

By finding what works for you, you will be able to optimize your performance, be that in school, work, sports, business or just life. I am not saying that you must work as hard as you can 100% of the time — you don't have to. What I am trying to do is to help you learn the difference between being lazy and being focused. Both require rest, but recovery is focused rest. As we have already seen in the section on time perspectives (page 31), its not ideal to spend every second of your life in the present moment or in the past or future for that matter, you need to plan for the future and learn from the past. Recovery is doing what you can in this present moment so that you are prepared for the future. This means that you can have optimum performance all the time.

Remember:

▶ Recovery is focused while rest is laziness.
▶ Rest can be enjoyable but not always beneficial.
▶ Preparation is important to recovery of any type.
▶ Your body will adapt, so rest less and recover more.
▶ Rest is still okay — sometimes.

DOING IT THE WRITE WAY

▶ Each of these ideas can help you create the future of your dreams.

▶ To achieve anything great, you must do the correct things on a daily basis.

▶ These are only ideas that will help; if you don't believe they will, you don't have to use them.

▶ Gratitude gives a balance and balance is amazing.

▶ Work on filling your mind with the great things it needs to hear; it will help you in the future.

The write stuff

Putting my thoughts and concerns down on paper has always been important for me, and writing this book has helped greatly in changing things that I need to change about myself. I'm not saying that you need to write a book to change your life but I would suggest doing some of the following exercises and games to help create a new outlook.

A letter to yourself

As already mentioned, a letter to yourself can definitely change your belief system and your entire outlook on the world. Below is a one-paragraph sample of what I think this letter should look like:

I am committed 100% to my process of improvement. I am improving daily in my mind, body and spirit. I am grateful for every day that I have. My days are my life in miniature, and as I live my days I live my life. I am excited about where I am going in my life and I have no other option but to succeed. I have a bank account that resembles $2,000,000 and I have every possession that I have ever dreamed of (list these possessions — cars, houses, boat, etc). What I am doing with my life is extraordinary and I am excited to be a part of the change that I want to see in the world.

As you can see, this is helping to manifest thoughts and beliefs that can only help you become who you want to become.

You don't have to list any physical or material possessions at all. If it is love and care that you want then write about that. You tailor your letter to you, just the same way you tailor your life to help meet your goals. Keep in mind that this letter is only useful if you are willing to put in the effort to achieve everything in it.

Gratitude journal

A gratitude journal is simple. You just keep track each day of anything that you are grateful for. The reason you do this is to bring some appreciation to the simple things in life. It's a simple concept but not many people do it, and it has the ability to help you attract whatever it is that you want into your life. You can have this wherever you want, on sticky notes, on your phone or in a journal that you keep. Just be sure you can access it easily. An example of this journal is:

▶ I am grateful today for my family and friends.
▶ Thank you for the clothes I have on my back.
▶ I appreciate the opportunities that I have encountered today.

123

▶ My lunch was beautiful, thank you.

As you can see, these simple acts of appreciation can help you see how lucky we are to have what we have. Try this gratitude journal to bring awareness and even more happiness into your life.

Daily achievement journal

The daily achievement journal is incredible and by far my favorite type of journal. The idea behind this is that it gives you the realization that, "I'm doing something today that is helping me achieve my goals", and it also helps you keep focused on what you need to do next in order to keep moving forward. On the facing page is an example of how to lay out your journal.

As you can see, this journal is completely positive and focused on success. Everything you are doing is helping you achieve the goals that you've set for yourself, and each of the things that you accomplish each day is continuously moving you closer to achieving your dreams. Just remember, don't think that once you achieve your dreams and have everything you want to have that you will necessarily be happy. The journey is the exciting part, and that's what you ought to enjoy.

124 In my own experience, these three writing rituals have

SAMPLE JOURNAL			
Achievement	**Why?**	**Next action**	**Further progress**
Got up at 5 am	I am trying to change a bad habit of sleeping in late	Repeat this tomorrow	Stay focused on getting up at 5 am and soon it will become a habit
Worked out	Trying to get in better shape and cut body fat	Eat healthily and train hard tomorrow	I will soon be in the shape that I desire
Read two new chapters of my current book	I am trying to educate myself	Keep notes and main points on everything that I do	Finish this book and be more knowledgeable on the subject I am learning about

changed my life. They have changed the way I think and the way I perceive situations. The letter to myself helps me stay focused and it gives me beliefs that I never would have had. It reinforces self-talk and erases self-doubt. It has been a vital tool in my life.

125

The gratitude journal has just made life simpler. It has cleared away the rubbish and made me grateful for everything. Gratitude has also made me aware of other people's actions and thinking and how they perceive the world. I know many people who have all the material possessions in the world and are still unhappy and they believe the world is against them. Separate yourself from these people, but also be grateful for them too because they bring awareness to your mind and clarity to your thinking. The achievement journal is something I write just before I go to bed. I write in three to five achievements that I have done that day. This reinforces your belief in your work ethic and it also has your brain focusing subconsciously on your further progress, or what you will do tomorrow.

"We rise or fall to the level of our conversation."
— **Robin Sharma,** author of *The Monk Who Sold His Ferrari*

The purpose of all of this is to help you believe that you are already a successful person. Keep up the good work, and I hope that some of my ideas have inspired you to become a more productive person.

AFFIRMATIONS: SOME EXAMPLES

Affirmations / Gratitude

▶ Thank you for waking me up this morning.

▶ Today will be a great day.

▶ I will stay in the present as much a possible today.

▶ I am the master of my mind and my life.

▶ My goals will come easy to me provided I do the work.

▶ Thank you.

▶ I am grateful for everything that I have in my life.

▶ Like attracts like. Today I will be grateful, abundant, caring and hard working. These will all lead me to where I want to go.

▶ I am the master of my future.

▶ Circumstances are irrelevant; my happiness comes from within.

▶ I live my life in a state of awareness. Awareness of my surroundings, my self-talk and my actions.

▶ Hard work is much more important than talent.

▶ I am extremely talented, but where I excel is through my hard work.

▶ Today is another opportunity to be the best that I can be and I am grateful for that.

▶ What I think today will shape my tomorrow. Today I am choosing to think great thoughts.

▶ I will live today and not merely exist.

▶ My invisible power is my mind. I am in total control and I am powerful.

▶ The world is a beautiful place when you accept the things you have no control over.

▶ The one thing I have control over is myself and that's all I will try to control.

Insert you name in the blank space:

My name is _____ and I thank you for giving me the opportunity of another beautiful day. My days are my life in miniature; as I live my days, so I live my life. I am going to do today what others won't, simply because I want to achieve great things. I am extremely humbled by the gifts that I have received from the world. I will live today in a state of awareness. I am aware of my thoughts and also my actions. I am improving each and every day. Today I will give something back to the world and I will say "Thank You" at every opportunity that I get. "Thank You" gives me a greater sense of clarity and it also brings me back to earth. With every moment comes a new opportunity to improve and I choose to improve every moment. Thank you for this new day! I am extremely grateful!

Inspiring books

The Success Principles (TM by Jack Canfield and Janet Switzer (HarperCollins).

The Noticer by Andy Andrews (Thomas Nelson).

Golf is a Game of Confidence by Dr Bob Rotella with Bob Cullen (Pocket Books/Simonsays).

Golf is Not a Game of Perfect by Dr Bob Rotella with Bob Cullen (Pocket Books/Simonsays).

The Big Miss by Hank Haney (Crowne Archetype).

Mike Tyson: Undisputed Truth by Mike Tyson with Larry Sloman (HarperCollins).

Rich Dad Poor Dad by Robert T. Kiyosaki (Plata Publishing).

The Talent Code by Daniel Coyle (Bantam Books).

Get Things Done by Robert Kelsey (Capstone).

Steve Jobs by Walter Isaacson (Little, Brown).

As a Man Thinketh by James Allen (Sublime Books).

The Alchemist by Paolo Coelho (Editora Rocco Ltd).

The Monk who Sold his Ferrari by Robin Sharma (Harper Collins).

Inspiring links

Killingsworth, Matthew A, and Gilbert, Daniel T: http://news. harvard.edu/gazette/story/2010/11/wandering-mind-not-a-happy-mind/

"All it takes is 10 mindful minutes" – Ted Talk by Andy Putticomb: http://www.ted.com/talks/andy_puddicombe_all_it_takes_is_10_mindful_minutes?language=en

"Your mind is a flashlight" – Ted Talk by Bodhin Kjolhede: https://www.youtube.com/watch?v=upNONoxskiw

Michael Jordan, Hall of Fame speech – https://www.youtube.com/watch?v=XLzBMGXfK4c

"Time Perception" – Ted Talk by Philip Zimbardo: http://www.ted.com/talks/philip_zimbardo_prescribes_a_healthy_take_on_time?language=en

***

If you would like to know more about me, please visit *www.danielbrennan.eu* or *www.uyplifestyle.com*.

Dedication

How can I dedicate a book to one particular person or one series of events? I don't believe I can. I could write a whole book thanking people and talking about events that continually added to my curiosity, but that's not what this book is about. This book is about you, the reader.

I would like to thank everyone who has a part to play in my life, good and bad. You have all helped shape me. To my parents, you have provided me with everything I could ever need. Thank you. I love you both.

I want to dedicate this book to all those amazing people who are curious about the world we live in and step out of their comfort zone and work hard at something they love. I salute you.

Lastly, with a portion of the profits from this book being donated to charities to help raise awareness of suicide and mental illness, I would like to dedicate this book to all of those in need. Although it may not seem like it, there are people out there who are willing to help. If this book can inspire one son or daughter, husband or wife, mom or dad, it will have served its purpose. Thank you.